BASIC FLY FISHING

for the

REASONABLY COMPETENT

ISBN 13: 978-0-692-57894-0

www.bigblackfootriverkeeper.org
joconnell@blackfoot.net

BIG BLACKFOOT

BASIC FLY FISHING

for the

REASONABLY COMPETENT

by Jerry O'Connell

Dedicated to my sweet Deborah,
who patiently put up with me while
I struggled to write this book.

FOREWORD

Trout don't live in ugly places. They also don't live in dirty water. As the executive director of The Big Blackfoot Riverkeeper, Inc. and a member of the internationally acclaimed Waterkeeper Alliance, I revere clean water and constantly seek ways to make more of it.

By buying this book, you are taking a small step to help make your waters cleaner. Ten percent of this book's proceeds will be donated to these organizations to help in the fight against pollution as we strive to protect and restore our waters and the critters that thrive in them.

– Jerry O'Connell

CONTENTS

Foreword

Introduction

Chapter 1
Why We Fly Fish   13

Chapter 2
Fish   19

   Where Are They?
   What Are They Eating?
   When Are They Eating?

Chapter 3
The Essential Tools   31

   The Rod
   The Reel
   Fly Line, Leaders, Tippets and Backing
   The Perfect Rig for the Beginner
   Other Stuff You'll Need

Chapter 4
The Essential Techniques   61

   The Only Knots You Need to Know
   The Art of the Cast
   Fly Line Management

Chapter 5
All About Insects   87

    Basic Bug Stuff: Latin-free Entomology
    Anatomy of an Artificial Fly
    Presenting the Fly
        Dry Flies
        Nymphs
        Wet Flies and Streamers

Chapter 6
Getting to the fish   109

    Row v. Wade
    You Have a Fish on the Line – Now What?

Chapter 7
Fly Fishing Etiquette   125

Chapter 8
Fly tying   131

Chapter 9
Conclusion   135

Appendix
Essential Equipment Check List   138

About the Author   139

INTRODUCTION

"In our family, there was no clear line between religion
and fly fishing."

– A River Runs Through It

B ECAUSE YOU'VE PICKED UP THIS BOOK, YOU'RE PROB-
ably a reasonably competent person. I think I am, too.
So why do we have to read books written for dummies to
learn new stuff? Unfortunately, without a "*<Something>
For Dummies*" option, we too often are limited to boring
tomes written by boring people for a bored audience.

Fly fishing literature deserves better. Fly fishing is one
of humanity's great inventions. It combines the essential
elements of art, sport, philosophy, aesthetics and suste-
nance into a peaceful and harmonious pastime. It's a simple concept, and yet at the same time it can be incredibly
complex. Like all the great pastimes, there's always more
to learn and ways to improve. This book is intended to
start you on your way, without insulting your intelli-
gence, and with enough basic fly fishing knowledge to
give you a legitimate shot at becoming addicted.

So let's get on with the learning, but without the Dummy overtones and definitely without elitist undertones.

CHAPTER 1

Why We Fly Fish When There Are Perfectly Good Worms About

"If you have never picked up a fly rod before, you will
soon find it is factually and theologically true that man
by nature is a damn mess."

– *A River Runs Through It*

MOST OF US WERE INTRODUCED TO FISHING IN OUR youth, standing on the edge of a pond fishing with bait. Usually we had an old rusty rod and reel and a coffee can full of worms dug up in the garden. The goal was to catch a fish—any fish—with no preference for species. Bullhead, bluegill, pumpkinseed, bass, carp and eel were all fair game, and getting any of these in hand provided an immediate thrill and a longer lasting sense of accomplishment.

Catching a fish is often one of the first great victories of our young lives. It transforms a child from just being a kid to being a *fisherman*. I've never known anyone who crossed that barrier and then put down their rod, never to fish again.

Certainly, some will later lose interest as other new experiences capture their interest. However, for a good number of kids at this stage (including yourself since you've picked up this book), this is just the start of a growing desire to advance their angling skills and achievements, a desire that will most likely end only when they exit the grand cosmic stage, toes up in a pine box.

The art of fishing, like many other pastimes, is not purely linear. As you gain knowledge and expertise, new options open up that will carry you in different directions. Artists first learn the basics before deciding on their favorite medium—oils, watercolors, sculpture, etc. Fishermen likewise have many directions to use their expanding fishing skills wherever their interests pull them—spin fishing, trolling and blue water big game fishing are just a few. And of course, there's fly fishing.

Let's clear the air up front—I hold no grudge with any of the non-fly fishing options. I've done them all, feel reasonably competent with them all and have thoroughly enjoyed them all. I will not make any attempt to argue for one over the other. You'll hear enough of that from virtually every fisherman you run into along the way, and you will have no problem voicing your own biases without my help.

However, if you've made it this far, you probably fall into that segment of the fishing world who senses that fly fishing may be their destiny. If so, welcome to a pastime with the potential to be so enjoyable that it requires a cautionary caveat—if left unchecked, fly fishing can consume everything in its path, including retirement savings, spouses, offspring and good friends.

Fly fishing, like most good things in life, is at its best when done in balance with the other loves of your life. Proceed with caution.

Enough with the legal disclaimers—let's get into it.

Why fly fish?

Originally, fly fishing was invented to catch trout. Trout feed almost exclusively on insects. Most of these are small and don't lend themselves to being threaded on a hook like a night crawler.

NOTE: Because of its historic connection to trout, this book is written with trout assumed to be your initial goal. Should you have other ideas for your piscatorial targets, be they bass, salmon, steelhead or carp, the lessons herein still apply.

Artificial flies were developed to replicate these little bugs, tying various parts of chicken feathers onto hooks to look vaguely like the local bugs. This presented another problem—the little artificial fly was too light to throw any distance with existing fishing methods in vogue at that time that involved heavier baits and weights.

Thus was born the art of fly fishing. The fly rod, a relatively long and flexible whip made from cane, was attached to a thick silk line heavy enough to be whipped through the air and tossed onto the water without need of a heavy weight on the end. Instead, the feathery fly was tied to a thin thread which was then tied to the end of the silk line, allowing the fly to float gently onto the water's surface like an insect.

Thus was also born the snobbery of fly fishing. Within moments of catching his first trout, that first fly fisherman put his nose in the air as he walked past his comrades and back to the pub to brag about his accomplishments.

Today, silk line has been replaced by exotic polymers, cane has been replaced by graphite and flies are tied with all sorts of strange materials. But the essence of fly fishing has not changed—it rewards the fisherman in direct proportion to their ability to weave together the elements of opportunity, knowledge, expertise, grace and patience.

Done reasonably well, fly fishing not only improves the odds of catching a fish, it also imparts a sense of intimate connection to, and integration of, the many elements that surround the fisherman in the process. While focusing on the fish in the water, the insects in the air and the movement of the current, gradually the mundane and troublesome issues of day-to-day life fade as you drop into what many feel is a zen-like state of peaceful contemplation. It lingers long after you've left the water, and each time a little bit more of it sticks with you forever. That is a good thing.

This altered state is perfectly described in the words of Norman Maclean*, author of *A River Runs Through It*. In the book's final paragraph, he writes *"All existence fades to a being with my soul and memories and the sounds of the Big Blackfoot River and a four-count rhythm and the hope that a fish will rise."*

---

*Author's note: I find myself quoting from *A River Runs Through It* often. As one of our greatest 20th century American writers, Norman Maclean has woven a literary tapestry whose warp and weft are made of his elegantly sparse writing style coupled with his intimate understanding of the essence of fly fishing. Do yourself a great favor and pick up a copy of this landmark work and read it every few years. It is good for the soul.

CHAPTER 2

Fish

Where Are They?

"I had no choice but to cast into the willows if I wanted
to know why fish were jumping in the water all around
me except in this hole, and I still wanted to know,
because it is not fly fishing if you are not looking for
answers to questions."

– A River Runs Through It

Rivers and Streams

FISH ARE EXTRAORDINARY CONSERVATORS OF ENERGY.
There is very little food value in an insect, so a trout
has to expend less energy getting it than it receives from
eating it.

In moving water, the trout prefers to save energy by
staying stationary while waiting to grab chow as it flows
by. To do that, a trout positions itself where there is little
or no current. That is often behind or directly in front
of a rock, in a quiet eddy or on the quiet seam between
two merging currents. In these holding waters, a trout
can remain immobile with only the occasional flicker of
a fin while keeping an eye on the upstream water, always
looking for its next micro-snack.

When a bug appears, the trout waits till it is moving
into its strike zone and then, with a quick flip of its tail,

shoots out into the current to grab the tidbit, then turns and coasts right back to its starting point.

By watching the water's movements, you will notice subtleties that identify likely trout hangouts. Exposed rocks create obvious eddies behind them, but submerged rocks and even undulations in the bottom can produce good hang-outs as well. Also, when a current splits and then rejoins downstream, the point of rejoining often has some holding spots, usually occupied by a fish or two.

Another good indicator to look for is where the currents have accumulated surface materials—foam, dead bugs, etc. Where there's highly visible foam, there's also harder-to-spot dead bugs. And where there's dead bugs, there's trout. Fish the foam.

To visualize these pointers, check out the two rivers on the next page. See how many good fish holding locations you can spot. On the page after that, you'll find those photos with all the good holding locations marked with a green star (feel free to cheat by looking ahead to see them all marked for you—there's no penalty points for that).

As you'll see, a relatively small stretch of water could have dozens of locations that could each be holding a few fish. You could spend an hour or more in either of these spots, working each holding area with a variety of flies until you hit the jackpot.

[*I can speak from experience on both of these locations as I've fished all those holding areas on many occasions, spending at least an hour every time and never getting bored (and only skunked once). The first is Montana's Big Blackfoot River and the other is Connecticut's Farmington River. Both are wonderful places to lose yourself for a day.*]

Still Waters—Lakes and Ponds

Unlike streams and rivers, lakes and ponds have little or no current to move the food past the trout, so the trout have to move past the food—that is, they need to swim around. There is still very little protein in each bug, so trout need to conserve energy while swimming through the water from one snack to the next. That means they move slowly, with only the occasional flick of the tail to keep up headway.

Several factors influence where trout will do most of their feeding:

1. There has to be food in the area. A lake-based fish's food supply comes from three directions—the bottom, the top, and the edges. On the bottom, it is found in the benthic layer of the water body (the upper inch or so of the bottom where the majority of aquatic critters live). Terrestrial insects (moths, grasshoppers, etc.) land on the surface, and worms, beetles and aquatic insects can be found along the lake's edge.

2. Water temperature—trout don't like warm water, and anything above about 70F will be avoided. During daylight hours, a lake's surface can warm up quickly, moving fish lower in the water column as they seek more pleasant temperatures.

3. Security—trout in shallow water are easy to spot and catch by predators like eagles and ospreys and bigger fish, so they'll avoid any shallow water that lacks a quick escape route.

So, taking all of these factors in account, the logic to determine where to put your fly is simple. If the fish are feeding in deep water at the bottom, you're screwed. If they're feeding off the top but out too far from shore, you're equally screwed (unless you have a boat handy). This leaves you with fishing waters shallow enough that trout can see your fly from their position near the bottom, but deep enough to be cooler and out of range of predators.

The good news is that this means you can fish most lakes from shore, casting out far enough to put your fly in water between 4-10' deep. Typically, your biggest problem will be keeping your fly out of the bushes and trees behind you.

When fishing still waters, you can fish with flies that move (wet flies, streamers) to increase your chances of getting it near a trout—they are very good at spotting movement through the water.

If you are fishing a dry fly, lightly jerk the fly a couple times a minute to create movement and ripples that will bring over fish in the area to check out your fly.

A nice thing about lake and pond fishing is that fish tend to be less selective because still waters usually have less food than moving waters—beggars can't be choosers. Another plus is you can set your cooler down on the bank for those times when you need a break. Not only does the cooler keep your beer cold, it makes a nice seat while you enjoy your brew.

So if you have still water nearby, there's no reason to not go out and give it a try.

What Are They Eating?

This is one of the great mysteries of fishing. On any particular stream or river, there may be several hatches of insects happening simultaneously. The trout are rising all over the water, but which insect are they eating?

First, let's define a few terms before confusion reigns. A *hatch* occurs when aquatic insects decide it's time to convert from their water-bound morphology to their airborne body style. This is known as metamorphosis, and most aquatic insect species tend to do it en masse. One moment nothing's happening, then suddenly the air could be filled with flying insects. That's a hatch. On many waters, several hatches of different insects can be happening at the same time.

While they are in mid-metamorphosis, many of these insects are resting on the surface of the water, waiting for the transition to complete itself. Later, after they've flown and mated, some will return to the surface to lay eggs, and all will soon land on the surface one final time when they run out of gas and die. Fish love to eat these bugs on the surface, either when coming or going. When they do, you can see the fish splashing and leaving expanding rings of ripples (a "rise form") behind. When fish are doing this, they are *rising*.

Nobody has figured out why, but trout in one pool might be eating mayflies, while just a few yards upstream they might be only eating caddisflies. And they could easily switch from one to the other on a moment's notice, seemingly at a whim.

Before you decide which fly to use, you should notice the kinds of flies that are on the water and in the air. Are they caddis? Mayflies? How big are they? What color are they? Answering these questions accurately when you're rummaging through your fly selections looking for the perfect imitation will greatly improve your chances of catching trout.

Next, watch where trout are rising (*if* they are rising) to figure out which kind of insect they're eating. Be forewarned—this is an imperfect science at best, since a trout's rise could be right by both an emerging caddis nymph alongside a dead mayfly. Which one is it eating, or did it eat a third bug you can't see?

If there are no fish rising, it doesn't mean there are no fish *feeding*. They are probably feeding but at that moment they are preferring food that's below the surface. They could be eating the same bugs you see flying around, but ones that are in a different life cycle than their airborne kin. Which means you need to start looking through your collection of nymph flies (relax—we'll explain this later).

The whole process of choosing the right fly to fit the conditions is at best a fairly inaccurate guessing game so patience again applies (this is another reason for the old saw "*that's why it's called fishing and not catching*").

Once you think you've figured out the answers, it's back to trial-and-error. Pick a fly that is styled after what seems to be the right hatch, matching as best you can both the size and color. If it works, great. If nothing goes for it after a dozen or so casts, try another size/color/style.

Here's a very important point—*don't hesitate to change flies if one isn't working.* Every time you make a change you are not only increasing your chances of success, you are learning a little piece of knowledge that steadily builds up body of work that turns you into a seasoned and competent fly fisherman.

NOTE: If you're feeling a bit lost with this arcane insect terminology (nymph, caddis, mayfly, emerger, hatches, etc.), fear not! Bugs are covered in an upcoming chapter, written specifically for non-entomologists like yourself. And there isn't a single Latin word in the whole chapter.

When Are They Eating?

"I often do not start fishing until the cool of the evening.
Then in the Arctic half-light of the canyon, all existence
fades to a being with my soul and memories and the
sounds of the Big Blackfoot River and a four-count
rhythm and the hope that a fish will rise."

– *A River Runs Through It*

Fish feed all the time, but feed more aggressively under
certain conditions. There are some generalizations that
you can use to increase your chances of catching trout.

First generalization—like virtually every other aspect of
fly fishing, there are no *rules,* just varying levels of prob-
ability that any piece of advice is accurate. No matter
how convincing somebody's logic sounds, it will never be
totally accurate. So with that, here are some more generalizations that will be true some of the time:

Time of day: Trout don't feed much during nighttime
because it's harder to see food. While fish don't sleep,
they do use the night hours to conserve energy. Generally, this means when the sun comes up, they're hungry
and on the feed.

As the day progresses, the sun gets higher and that
means fish sink lower in the water column. Not only can

trout get sunburn if they stay too close to the surface, the brighter conditions make them more visible to predators like ospreys and eagles. Thus, dry fly fishing tends to slow down during mid-day, while drifting a nymph near the bottom still produces fish.

As the sun moves lower in the afternoon sky, trout begin to look up for food again. The cooler air also triggers a higher number of insect hatches which helps put the trout in a feeding mood. Finally, the last part of the day before darkness arrives is often called the "magic hour" as trout go on their final rush to pig out before another night of energy conservation.

Weather: Fish don't mind rain—they're already wet. Trout don't mind heat, as long as the water doesn't get too warm. What seems to put trout off their feeding cycles is *change*. If a cold front comes through, fishing will often turn off for a day or two. Whether it's the change in air pressure, wind direction or air temps, something about it can get them off the feed. But not always.

Moon phase: This has some fairly measurable and predictable impact on fishing. It's not because they are somehow cosmically connected to the Solar System (they may be, but there's a simpler explanation). When the moon is full and the sky is clear, it's bright enough for fish to feed more at night than usual. That means they don't have the need to eat as much during the day as they normally would, thus fishing during a full moon is generally less productive than other times.

Likewise, during a new moon (and during any overcast night), their night feeding is at its absolute minimum. By morning, they will be just that much hungrier. Or not.

CHAPTER 3

The Essential Tools

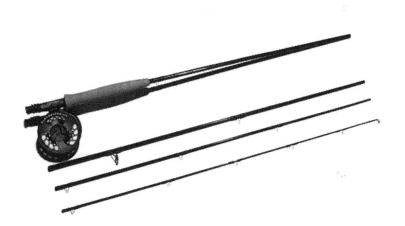

The Rod

"If someone called it a pole, my father looked at him as
a sergeant in the United States Marines would look at a
recruit who had just called a rifle a gun."

– A River Runs Through It

FIRST OF ALL, IT'S A ROD, NOT A POLE. A POLE IS A BIG
log covered with creosote that holds up power lines.
A rod, on the other hand, is a delicately balanced work of
art that connects you to the river and hopefully the fish
within it.

Fly rods come in many sizes and flavors, depending on
what you're fishing for, where you're fishing for it and
how much you can invest. One should look at this as
an investment for two reasons—a fly rod and its owner
often develop a near-surreal emotional attachment to
each other, and at the high end a fly rod can carry a significant price tag.

Basically, there are three important criteria for a fly
rod—length, weight and its construction materials.

Length

Fly rods typically range in length from 7' to 9'. There is a whole class of much longer rods designed for spey casting, but since that's an advanced style of fly fishing normally reserved for more experienced anglers, we'll leave the spey casters to themselves while we stick with the 7'-9' range here.

All other factors being equal, a longer rod will let you cast a longer distance. This is helpful when fishing larger waters and when there's plenty of room to cast. Thus you'll find most fishermen in the big waters of western rivers using 9' rods. However, if you're fishing on smaller waters like those found in the Northeast, the narrow brooks and surrounding bushes and shrubs make a long cast both difficult and unnecessary. These conditions fit perfectly to a 7' rod. If you fish both small and big waters but just have one rod, an 8' is a fine compromise that can perform reasonably well in all conditions.

Weight

In the old days of cane rods, the actual weight of a rod was important because some of those old rods could be downright heavy. A heavy rod makes for strenuous casting and sore wrists and arms by day's end, so rod makers always specified how many ounces each rod weighed.

These days, modern materials are making stronger and lighter rods that minimize a rod's weight so it's no longer a big factor. Today, the term *weight* has redefined itself to describe the weight of the fly line a rod is designed to carry. Line weight is classified by a numbering scheme ranging from 1 to 14. The lower the number, the thinner and lighter the line. Light lines (1-3 weight) can be cast with a delicate, short rod and are great for small, tight waters. Mid-weight lines (4-7 weight) are good for a wide variety of conditions and species. Heavy lines (8-14 weight) are more specialized for larger game fish. You can find more details about the various lines and their uses in the Lines chapter.

Flex

Rods are not only rated by length and weight, but also by the amount of flex it displays, also called *action.*.

"Slow" rods have lots of flex when you cast, which give them a sensitive feel—some think of it as *finesse*— that can deliver soft, accurate casts but get somewhat mushy when you try for distance.

"Fast" rods are made stiffer to put maximum power into a cast resulting in longer distances and best able to punch your fly into a strong wind. The tradeoff comes with a reduction in feel and finesse, particularly when making shorter casts.

Between these extremes are a host of rods designed to capture a happy medium between power and feel. These go by the terms "medium fast," "moderate flex," etc. .

As with so many other facets of fly fishing, there is no right or wrong choice here, so just do what feels most comfortable to you. Since it's hard to judge the casting ability of a rod by waggling it in the fly shop, I suggest getting a medium to medium-fast action for your first rod and worry about other refinements next season.

Construction Materials

The first serious fly rods were made of bamboo, commonly called cane. Making a cane rod is a tedious, labor-intensive process that splits the cane into strips, then planes each into a trapezoidal shape so that six of them glued together form a hollow shafted rod 'blank'. After gluing them together, they are heated with a flame to strengthen the rod and to achieve its desired flex. Cane rods are still available today, and the best are revered as fine works of art. They also can require a second mortgage, so most of us opt for less expensive options.

Fiberglass came into favor in the 1950's as a good alternative to cane. Inexpensive, strong, and light, "glass" rods quickly became the standard rod material. Then in 1973, The Fenwick Corporation introduced the first graphite rod and the fishing world changed forever. This new material made a much lighter rod than those of glass or cane, and allowed rod makers to design a rod's stiffness to fit a variety of personal casting styles.

Advances in manufacturing and in the graphite itself since that time has resulted in rods today that truly can become a natural extension of the fisherman's arm without necessarily separating the fishermen from their wallets.

Graphite is now the new standard in fly rods. Since graphite rods are a bit fragile, a tiny nick in the finish can create a weak point that may suddenly snap your rod at which point it becomes instantly worthless. Because of this, not only is graphite the new standard, so is the manufacturer's lifetime replacement warranty. Make sure your rod maker offers one because odds are you'll be breaking your graphite rod more than once in its lifetime.

While graphite represents the leading edge, in the last few years fiberglass rods have had a bit of a comeback using lighter binding resins to produce a rod with nice feel, a relatively bulletproof body and a more digestible price tag. They're worth a look.

Miscellaneous

Rods are made up of several segments so that they can be taken apart and carried with ease. The 2-piece rod was the standard for years, but improvements to the segment connectors (ferrules) have made 3- and 4-piece rods feasible without a loss of sensitivity that older ferrule designs imparted. A 4-piece 9-foot rod can fit into a 27" rod case, which can then fit under your car seat and in any airplane overhead storage bin. So, unless you want to be a traditionalist, make your first rod a 4-piece.

The Reel

There is an endless selection of reels to satisfy any fisher-man's tastes. You can find a used but functional Pflueger Medalist reel for $20 on the Internet. You can also pick up a Joe Saracione hand-made, rubber-sided, nickel-plated trout reel for $3,500. Both can work equally well when catching a fish.

Unless you are fishing for *big* fish, your reel is primarily there to store fly line. You don't need a fancy drag (hell, you don't need *any* drag) to catch most fresh water fish. You don't need a reel made from gold-anodized titanium. At the same time, you probably don't want a crappy reel made out of plastic either.

So, what do you really need? Well, not a whole lot. That $20 used Pflueger Medalist is a good choice (I have one I found in a Montana pawn shop for $12 twenty years ago and it still works fine). If you want to step it up a touch, an inexpensive large-arbor reel is a good alternative.

Small arbor reel   Large arbor reel

(Pflueger Medalist)   (Sage 4600)

Large arbor means the spool holding the line has a larger-than-average diameter, allowing you to reel in more line with each turn of the handle. Nice feature, but not essential.

I personally like the look of a more traditional reel, so I only use large arbor reels on my big-fish rods. It is all a matter of personal taste and preference.

On the off chance you are beginning with saltwater fishing, your reel choice becomes more important. Any reel used in saltwater must be anodized, which makes it resistant to corrosion. Without that, your reel will permanently seize up within days of reeling in line dripping with saltwater. Also, you'll need a reel with a decent drag system, which allows a big fish to run line off your reel while maintaining enough resistance to keep the line tight and the hook in place.

As you might guess, these essential features can add significant cost to the reel. A decent saltwater reel will set you back at least a few hundred bucks, which is another good reason to start your fly fishing career in fresh water.

Now that I've made it clear that a simple, basic reel is all you need for most situations, here's the twist. The reality is most fishermen develop close, intimate feelings for their reels. As one gains experience, you may find the subtle, sonorous click and silky action of some of the more expensive reels irresistible. Like a golfer with a putter collection, there's a good chance you'll eventually have many more reels than necessary.

If your wallet allows it, don't fight the urge. Reels are neat.

Fly Line, Leaders, Tippets and Backing

Unlike other fishing techniques, fly fishing requires a line made up of a somewhat complex set of elements that work together to get your fly to the fish and hopefully your fish eventually into the net. These are the four components that make up your line.

—

Fly line: The whole purpose of fly fishing is to throw a near-weightless object a fair distance with reasonable accuracy. The fly line is the key to doing this effectively. The line's weight provides the momentum needed to throw the near-weightless fly that fair distance.

There are a wide variety of fly lines available to deal with every situation. Some are made to float, some to sink slowly, some to sink quickly. Some are thin and silk-like, some are as thick as shoelaces.

To deal with all these variations, the fly line industry has settled on a classification system to make it easy to select the right line. First, the diameter (and thus the weight) of a line is classified by a number ranging from 1 to 14. A 1-weight line has a very thin diameter and results in a lightweight line that lets you make delicate and precise casts but only works well for shorter casts made with delicate rods. At the other end of the spectrum, a 14-weight line is very thick and typically used with a heavy duty rod with the flex of a tire iron to lob big gaudy wads of sparkly plastic ribbons tied around a gaff-sized hook at large pelagic fish like sailfish and marlin.

In addition to thickness, there are variations in the taper of the line from its thickest area to its thinner end points. A fly line can be "double taper" where each end is tapered a bit and the middle portion is thicker. This allows the line to be swapped end-for-end after heavy use begins to break down the used part of the fly line, effectively doubling its life. The alternative is to get a "weight forward" line with a more complex taper at one end to optimize casting. This cannot be swapped end-for-end and thus has a shorter usable life than a double-taper, but the weight-forward line allows you to make a slightly more precise cast than a double-taper.

Double tapered lines are labeled "DT." Weight-forward lines are labeled "WF."

Finally, fly lines are designed to either float or sink. Floating lines are labeled—you guessed it—"F." Sinking lines are labeled "S."

Put it all together and you'll be able to make a bit more sense of the fly line display cabinet at your local fly shop. A WF-5-F is a weight-forward 5-weight floating line. A DT-7-S is a double tapered, 7-weight sinking line. Etcetera. Simple, no?

—

Leader: If you don't already know it, you'll soon discover that the eyelet on the fly's hook is much smaller than the diameter of the fly line. You can't tie one to the other. Plus, the fly line being relatively thick and very opaque makes it very visible to trout. Having it sticking out of what otherwise would look like a nice snack for a trout will squirrel the deal. Thus the need for a 'leader'. A leader is a length of clear, usually monofilament line that attaches to the end of the fly line. The leader is tapered so that it gets thinner as it approaches the far end where the fly will reside.

The leader manufacturing industry lacked the wisdom of the fly line makers when it comes to using a standard labeling system. Luckily, there aren't a whole lot of options to consider right now. Basically, your choices are the length of the leader and the thickness of the leader at its thin end. Leaders come in lengths ranging from 5' to 12'. While the shortest and longest versions have their place in the fishing world, 90% of your fishing can be done with a 9' leader. So keep it simple for now—just get yourself a 9-footer.

The second variable is the diameter of the thin end. Here a bit of a standard shows up. Leaders and 'tippets' (to be explained below) both use the same classification system to describe their diameter. Rather than repeat myself, I'll leave the details on this to the *Tippet* section.

One final clarification you may need when selecting your leaders. Most leaders today are sold as a single length of line, tapered from the butt end (the thick end that ties to the fly line) all the way to the thin part designed to tie directly to the fly. However, there are some leaders that come in two parts—the first part running from the butt section for most of the length of the leader with a loop at the other end. The second part of the leader is the "tippet" section with a loop in one end which will connect to the leader's end loop. Your fly is then tied to the end of the tippet.

There's a good reason for this replaceable tippet. Each time you cut off a fly and tie on another, you'll use up several inches of tippet. After a few hours of changing flies, you will have used up the thin section of a single-piece tapered leader and soon find you're trying to tie a fly to increasingly thicker, more visible and less delicate leader material. At that point you will need to either replace the entire leader with a new one (wasteful) or attach a new thin section of tippet to the now-shortened leader (the proper approach). The 2-part leader makes this an easy task.

—

Tippet: At the far end of the leader, the line needs to be thin enough to fit through the eyelet of your fly, and also be thin enough to be effectively invisible to the trout. To do this, there is a final segment of line, called the tippet, that forms the last 3' or so of the leader and is tied directly to the fly.

With a single-piece tapered leader, this is typically the last 3' of the leader. Two-part leaders come with a 3' tippet section that you connect to the heavier leader section with a simple loop-to-loop connection. These often come in an envelope with two or three extra tippet sections.

Tippets are the thinnest part—and the weakest link—in the whole system. The diameter (and thus strength) of the tippet you'll want to use depends on the size of fly and kind of fishing you are doing at the moment.

Tippets are classified by their diameter using an numerical rating scale ranging from 0X (very thick) to 8X (very thin). 8X tippets are hair-like in their diameter with a breaking strength of about 2 lbs. At the other end of the tippet spectrum, 0X can have a breaking strength of 30+ lbs. To get started, you'll be using tippets ranging from 3X to 6X. There are even bigger and stronger tippets for those inclined to catch sharks and other toothy critters, but we're only getting started—let's not worry about that heady stuff yet.

—

Backing: Fly lines usually come in 90'-100' lengths. Your reel, by comparison, may be capable of holding much more line. The result is the reel's spool will be barely half-filled once you wind on your fly line. This presents two problems. First, it takes many turns of the reel handle to retrieve your fly line because of the small diameter of the spool. Second, if you hook up with a strong fish that wants to run more than 100', you're out of luck. The solution to both of these situations is *backing*.

Backing is relatively thin but strong line, typically woven dacron, that is wound onto your reel before anything else. You want enough backing to fill the reel sufficiently so that when the fly line is tied to it and wound onto the reel, the reel is filled to its capacity.

With the proper amount of backing, a turn of the reel handle now retrieves much more line because of the increased diameter of the spool. Also, should a big fish take you for a 100'+ ride, your backing provides ample insurance that you'll not run out of line.

How do you know how much backing to put on before you tie on your fly line? Good question. Answer—you don't know and will probably guess wrong, waste a lot of time and get frustrated.

The simple solution is to bring your reel into your fly shop, buy the backing and ask them to put it on for you. They know how much you'll need and they have a machine to do it quickly. And unless they're a very unpleasant shop, they'll do it for free.

The Perfect Rig for the Beginner

The most common rods used for trout fishing are those designed for 3- to 7-weight lines. Of these, the single most common trout rod is a 9' 5-weight. Fly fishing shorthand lingo would describe this as a "9 for 5." With all these options, you'll almost certainly make a mistake if you buy your first rig unassisted, so seek guidance from your local fly shop staff when choosing that first rig.

Certainly, you could get a feathery 1-weight to use on a small Pennsylvania spring creek, but you'll spend most of the day plucking your fly from the willows behind you. You could also start with a 14-weight and go for tuna from the pitching deck of a sport fisherman miles off-shore, but you'll probably spend most of that day with your head over the side, laying down a chum slick for the benefit of the more seaworthy fishermen on the boat.

I don't recommend beginning your fly fishing experiences in either of these environments. Not only do they take special skills, they both offer very limited options on how to cast, where to cast and what to cast. This puts limits on how much you can learn and reduces the odds of starting out with a positive fly fishing experience.

Instead, I strongly advise beginners to start with a mid-sized rig with a floating fly line. The benefit of floating line is that it works for both floating and sinking flies, while sinking line won't work with floating flies. Also, being a bit lighter, floating lines are easier to cast.

Now take that rig out to some to some bigger water where there's plenty of room to cast and hopefully a reasonable quantity of fish in the water. There is almost always a nearby river, pond or lake that has at least a modicum of a sport fishing reputation.

I'm not suggesting you sneak into the state hatchery pond (although I do have friends that have had a ball doing so). Many towns have a park with a pond that allows fishing. Park ponds are great because they're usually surrounded with groomed grounds— there is no better place to cast then from a mowed lawn.

Ponds often have bass and bluegills which are easy prey to a fly. The lucky fisherman may find a public pond stocked with trout. Either way, the thrill of catching your first fish on a fly—be it bass, bullhead or brown trout— will stay with you for the rest of your life. I promise.

My first fish on a fly was a bluegill out of a New Jersey lake in 1959 using a fly I tied with a single white feather from my pet duck Chuckles and my mom's sewing thread. Ten years later, I caught my first trout on that same fly on Connecticut's Farmington River. Both fish are still vivid in my memory.

So, with this in mind, here is my recommendation for your first rig:

ITEM		*ESTIMATED COST*
Rod	9' 5 weight 4-piece medium-flex graphite rod	**$120-200**
Reel	a reel designed for 5-weight line	**$75-120**
Line	a basic 5-weight weight-forward floating line (WF-5-F)	**$60**
Leader	9' 4X	**$10**
Tippet	Three spools, one each of 3X, 4X, and 5X size	**$20**
Backing	One 100 yard spool of 30# backing	**$10**
Total rig		**$295-$420**

Other Stuff You'll Need

Now that you've got your rig squared away, you'll want to flesh out the rest of your outfit with essential and not-quite-essential items to help make your fly fishing experience a pleasant one.

The gear falls into three broad categories—*1)* things you need to help put flies on your line, *2)* things to help put fish on your line and *3)* things to keep your personal comfort and safety in line.

—

For Putting a Fly on Your Line

Nippers: This is the fisherman's version of nail clippers. Simple in design, they are essential to clip all sorts of stuff, including leaders, tippets and excess fly material (for turning a larger fly into a smaller fly 'on the fly'). You should keep this

handy by clipping it to a *zinger* hanging off your vest (see below).

Forceps: Also called Kelly clamps (and roach clips in some circles), these are lightweight pliers that serve many uses, most commonly to crimp the barb on a hook, to remove a fly from a fish's mouth and occasionally to remove your friend's fly from his thumb.

Retractors/Zingers: These hold your various tools (nippers, forceps, etc.) close at hand but out of the way. They have a clip on one end to attach your tool, a clip on the other end to attach to you and a retractable cord to pull it out of the way when not needed. Get several.

Floatant and holder: Assuming you'll be using dry flies, this is essential to keep a dry fly floating on top of the water. There are several styles, most common being a silicon gel in a small squeeze bottle. The holder lets you clip the floatant bottle to your zinger or to a loop on your vest.

Nontoxic split shot: Even if you plan to be a dry fly fisherman, you will occasionally want to fish a fly near the bottom. Split shot let you do that. Think of these as soft metal ball bearings with a slit in them. Place your leader into the slit, then crimp the metal closed using your forceps. You want to use only nontoxic shot because otherwise they'll be made of lead, which nobody wants in their waters for obvious reasons.

Strike indicators: When fishing beneath the surface, these allow you to see when a fish grabs your fly. These are NOT bobbers! Bobbers are for bait fishermen. We're better than that—we use *strike indicators*. There are many styles ranging from clip-on plastic colored bubbles (whose resemblance to those tacky bobbers is strictly a coincidence) to tufts of brightly colored wool or nylon. Visibility is the key to selecting the proper color. To each his or her own.

While we're on the subject, here's a fascinating fact—if fishing late in the evening with minimal light, the easiest indicator color to see is black!

Fly boxes: You need these to store your flies. These come in all sizes, shapes, styles and construction materials— plastic, metal, Styrofoam and even wood. How big and how many you need depends on your personal fly collection—some make do with a few dozen flies, others a few hundred. Plan accordingly and make sure your boxes are small enough to fit into your vest or fishing shirt pockets.

Spare leaders: Even though a leader can last all season, it's good to have a spare or two. You should always have at least one just in case. They weigh next to nothing, come in little envelopes and slip into any gear pocket.

Spare tippet spools: These small, thin spools carry anywhere from 10 to 30 yards of tippet. You'll want a set of these in the sizes you use most often. For typical trout fishing, that would be a spool (or two) each of 3X, 4X, 5X, and 6X. There are many good makers of tippet, but it will make your life easier if you get them all from the same manufacturer. Most design their spools to snap together so you can have a nice array of your most commonly used sizes all clipped together hanging on a zinger on your vest. Keep your spare spools in storage pockets in your vest.

Spool holder: This simple little device holds a set of tippet spools and has a clip on it to attach to your vest.

Knot tool: Not quite essential until you need to attach a new leader to your fly line when you're far from anyone who knows how to do it. Should that happen, you'll want this. They all come with a little instruction card covering the most common complicated knots in the plastic envelope with the tool. Keep it in your vest. Inevitably you will need it at some point, and having it will save the day.

Magnifiers: Unless you're one of the lucky ones that has 20/20 vision at all distances, you'll probably need these when tying on a fly. Basically, these are various forms of reading glasses. Some clip to the visor of your hat, some just hang around your neck (i.e., reading glasses). You might also consider using sunglasses with built-in magnifiers (see sunglasses below).

Mini flashlight/headlamp: Not really essential until you realize there are fish starting to rise all around you just as it's getting too dark to tie a fly onto your tippet. A light can save the day (or night). Some clip into a pocket with a goose neck light, some you wear on your head, some you just hold in your mouth. They all do the job, and it's a necessity for the "Magic Hour" when you'll be frantically changing flies in diminishing light trying to figure out what they're suddenly feeding on.

Vest/chest pack/lanyard: Obviously after getting this far in the gear list, you'll need some place to carry all this stuff.

The vest is the traditional garment for this, filled with bunches of various-sized pockets and storage areas with built-in zingers, clips and loops.

Should your preference be for a more minimalist approach, there are chest packs and over-the-shoulder sling packs that hold a lesser amount of gear but take a lesser amount of space. Lanyards are the next step toward minimalism, being a glorified necklace with bunches of clips to which you attach your essential tools (but not fly boxes). There is no correct choice—it's all personal preference.

—

For Putting a Fish on Your Line

Wading sandals/boots: River bottoms are always slippery, making wading footwear essential. While wool panels on the bottom of the sole make for excellent slip resistance, they also promote transfer of invasive species between watersheds. They're actually now banned in some states, and that trend is growing. Look at footwear with the new sticky rubber soles, some with removable cleats to increase grip, which are becoming the new standard.

Sandals and lightweight shoe styles work very nicely when water temperatures allow "wet wading." However, in spring and late fall when water is colder, waders become essential. Because of waders' rather thick neoprene booties, a boot specifically designed for waders is required. You can wear these wader boots without the waders in warmer weather as long as you get a pair of neoprene socks to make a good fit.

Waders: There are two basic styles, hip waders and chest waders. If you don't think you'll ever wade in water more than mid-thigh deep, hip waders are the way to go. They're light, cool, and don't take up much space in your closet or the back of the car.

If you wade into deeper water, you'll need chest waders. There was a time when neoprene chest waders were the rage, but they were hot and tough to put on and take off. Most waders now are made of lighter, looser, more comfortable and breathable material (Gore Tex, etc). They come with either a built-in boot or a neoprene booty that fits into a separate boot. Once again, personal preference prevails on which is best for you.

Wader belt: A wader belt cinches around your waist and over your waders and is only important when you slip and fall in. When (not *if*) that happens, the belt keeps water from filling your waders and thus improves your chances of ending the day with your buddies laughing at your clumsiness instead of mourning your passing. If your chest waders don't have a belt built into them, definitely get yourself one of these.

Wader patch kit: The breathable wader material requires a special patch to fix leaks. Most waders come with a patch kit stored in an inner pouch. If not, you can always pick one up at your local fly shop.

Landing net: Not an essential item, but this certainly makes landing a fish much easier for the uninitiated. Most nets these days are wood (although you can still find an aluminum one if you insist on looking tacky). The most important part is the netting material. Do

NOT get one made of knotted nylon or polypropylene, which injures fish by scraping off their protective slime. Your net should either be fish-friendly soft knotless nylon or rubberized netting material.

The net snaps to the back of your vest or to a loop on the back of your fishing shirt.

Landing net holder: Many nets come with an elastic loop on the handle to hook to the back of your vest. My advice—cut the elastic off as soon as you get it home and replace it with a holder that lets you hang the net handle-down off the back of your vest.

Why? One stroll through brush is all it takes to understand why that elastic loops are a bad idea. The netting will snag on a shrub as you walk, stretching the elastic out behind you to its maximum extension before the net rips out of the shrub and slams you in the back of the head. Ouch. Guaranteed.

Net holders let you safely grab the net off your back by the handle just by tugging it. Some use a magnet, others use a pressure-release clip. Since you're always fish-on when going for your net, the less effort and concentration required to get it in your hand the better. This is a nice little addition to your optional equipment list.

Hat: Nothing fancy here as long as your chapeau has a brim. A ball cap, cowboy hat, or anything in between works just fine. A dark underside on the brim is a plus, as this reduces reflective glare. The brim is essential to keep direct sunlight off your tender little eyeballs which helps immensely when trying to keep an eye on your fly on the water.

Polarized sunglasses: Clearly an essential item. Polarized lenses eliminate nearly all reflective glare off the water, letting you see well into the water column to sight fish, to see fish feeding on the surface and to follow your fly as it drifts along. There are some new and very cool ones being made with built-in magnifiers at the *top* of the lenses. Whoever thought of that deserves a big bonus.

—

For Your Personal Safety and Comfort

Wading staff: If you're over 50, you'll need this now or soon. Whatever it is that departs our bodies around that half century mark, the result is in an increased tendency to slip and fall into the river, particularly when there are witnesses. Most wading staffs telescope closed or fold up easily when not in use, hanging right off your belt. Swallow your pride and invest in one.

Rain gear: Go fancy with a breathable jacket designed for fishing or go cheap with a plastic poncho, but have it handy. Not sure if it's because of the climatic conditions or the fact that there are few fishermen around, but rainy days can make for great fishing.

UV protection: A tube of SPF30 should be in your vest— lips, ears and face can burn fast in the reflective light of a sunny day on the water. You can also get a UV buff, a balaclava-like head-and-neck mask that provides total protection from the sun. Just remember to take it off before you stop by the bank on your way home.

Fishing shirts: These are lightweight, quick drying nylon or cotton/nylon blend and loaded with pockets big enough for a fly box or two, your wallet and other essentials. Plus they look cool at the saloon after a day on the water.

Fishing pants: Like the shirts, these are light and quick-drying. Consider the ones with zip-off legs that let them convert to a pair of shorts. They also have good sized pockets with solid closures to insure valuable stuff doesn't float away.

Half-finger gloves: For fall, spring, and winter fishing, these can turn a cold-shortened half-day of fishing into a pleasant all-day affair. The open finger tips make for easy fly changes without having to remove the gloves.

Gear bag: If you travel any distance to your fishing destinations, this is a nice addition to hold all your gear and your lunch. These are usually breathable and waterproof, and come in many sizes to handle whatever amount of gear you take along with you.

Pocket knife: Who doesn't need one of these now and then? Whether it's a simple one-bladed affair or a full-blown Leatherman tool, a knife is a handy tool to have along.

Auto-inflating emergency personal floatation device (PFD): Some people say this is overkill. Those people have yet to slip into cold, deep, fast water in their waders. Once they do (and we all eventually do), they'll get

themselves a self-inflating PFD. Taking up no more space than a thick pair of suspenders, this could turn out to be a life saver. It uses a sodium bicarbonate plug that, when it gets wet, instantly triggers a CO_2 cartridge that inflates it to a full-size life preserver in just a few seconds.

Keep this in mind—spring is not only the opening of fishing season in most places, it's also when the water is high and cold. You'll be wearing waders and wading boots, neither of which are designed for swimming. Now picture yourself slipping and tipping into cold, fast moving water. Trust me—this gets ugly fast. You'll initially struggle in vain to regain your feet as the current knocks you down repeatedly as you get washed downstream. Only when you're nearly exhausted do you realize you're in trouble. Swimming is now your only option but with the heavy boots and water-filled waders, it's an exercise in futility. How does that auto-inflating PFD sound now?

I stress the *auto-inflating* based on past personal experience. A few years back a very good fishing companion was thrown from my raft into deep, fast waters. He was immediately pulled to the bottom and nearly drowned before he very luckily was washed into an eddy and was able to crawl out. Only then did he remember that he was wearing an inflatable PFD—but one that required him to pull a big yellow handle in front to inflate it. It was labeled "JERK" and thus became his nickname from that day forward.

Pocket flask: The perfect item to have after you've survived a spill and struggled to shore thanks to your auto-inflatable PFD. Toast your survival with a long draw on a smoky single malt!

CHAPTER 4

The Essential Techniques

The Only Knots You Need to Know

"To him, all good things—trout as well as eternal salvation—come by grace and grace comes by art and art does not come easy."

– A River Runs Through It

FOR REASONS UNKNOWN, FLY FISHERMEN HAVE DEVELoped a very long list of complicated knots to meet a fairly short list of situations. Put a handful of fly fishermen in a bar and before long they'll be name-dropping their favorite arcane knot as though anyone not using it is a fool. Surgeon's knot, nail knot, blood knot, needle knot, Albright knot, Palomar knot, Bimini twist—the list goes on ad nauseum.

The bad news is that most of them are difficult if not impossible to tie unless you do it all the time (like that guy in the fly shop that puts the backing on your fly reel). Knot tying books have drawings based on the theory that a picture is worth a thousand words, but knots are the exception to that rule. Good luck trying to replicate that in real life. It is not fun.

For the rare time you need one of the esoteric knots— say, a nail or needle knot to tie a new leader to your fly line (normally a once-a-season event)—get yourself a knot tying tool at any fly shop. They typically come with a handy instruction pamphlet. Should the need for one of these oddball knots arise while on the water, put down your rod, find a comfortable place to sit, pull out the tool and its instructions and go at it. You'll eventually get it done, but it will take some time and patience. Since these situations are rare occasions, we're not going to worry about these complicated knots here.

By the way, if you are in cell phone range on the water (and haven't yet learned that you always leave your phone in your car when you go fishing), there are some slick smart phone apps for knot tying that give some great visual help. I personally like *www.animatedknots.com* but there are new ones all the time.

All that being said, the good news is that for the vast majority of us, just two knots are all you need to get you through the typical season.

You need knots on a regular basis for two primary purposes: 1) tie on a fly, and 2) tie on a new section of leader and/or tippet. There are a variety of knots that do these tasks nicely, and each fisherman has their favorite. I've selected what I think are the simplest reliable knots for each of these situations. Both are easy. Try them out and pick whichever one fits your fingers and brain best.

Here's a good tip—once you find the ones you like, tie them ten times in a row while sitting in the comfort of your home. At that point, muscle memory should take over and you'll be able to tie these knots streamside quickly and without frustration.

Knots for Tying on the Fly

Improved clinch knot:

The "improved" clinch knot is just one extra step beyond a simple clinch knot, but it's a very important step. I learned this the first time I hooked up—and lost to a failed knot—a bonefish. My guide watched me tie on another fly with a simple clinch knot. "That's a good knot if you want to hook a bonefish" he said, "but if you want to *catch* a bonefish, tie an *improved* clinch knot." And he was right. I still lost plenty of bonefish, but at least not to a failed knot.

1. Put the leader through the hook's eye and pull about 5-6" of tippet through it (as you get better at this knot, you'll need less line.)

2. Wrap the *tag end* of the tippet (the part that has gone through the eye) 4-5 times around the *standing line* portion of the tippet (the part that runs back up to the rest of the leader).

3. Pass the tag end through the loop in the tippet between the eye and the first wrap on the standing line.

4. Now pass the tag end through the bigger loop you just created between the eye and the last wrap on the standing line (this is the step that makes it "*improved*").

5. Pull on the standing line while holding the tag end. Once pulled tight, snip off the tag end as close to the knot as possible.

NOTE: Before the knot tightens up, moisten the tippet in the knot area with a bit of water or saliva. This lubricates the line and prevents friction heat building up that can weaken the line.

Knots for Tying Tippet to Your Leader

Perfection Loop:

This knot will result in a small loop which can then be connected to another line with a similar loop in its end (explained a bit further on). It's the perfect way to connect a new length of tippet to your leader.

This may seem tricky the first time, but after tying it a few times you'll get the feel for it and you'll be able to do it in the dark. While this description assumes a right-handed person, just reverse it for lefties.

1. Hold the tippet between your right thumb and forefinger with about 5-6" of tag end sticking out to the left. Grasp the tag end with your left hand and form a clockwise loop and placing the line on top of the line laying between your thumb and forefinger.

    Grip the two between your thumb and finger. The loop should be about 1" in diameter with the tag end pointing to the left as it sticks out from under your thumb.

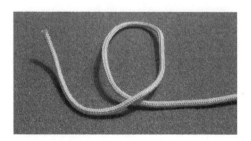

2. Grasp the tag end and make a second, *slightly smaller* loop so that the tag end passes behind the first loop. Bring the tag end around to the front of the first loop, again gripping it with the same fingers so the tag end now sticks out to the left.

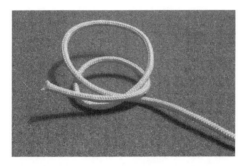

3. Pull the tag end to the right and between the first and second loops and place it between your fingers so it now points to the right.

4. With your left thumb and forefinger, reach through the first loop, grab the second loop and pull it toward you through the first loop. Continue to hold your right thumb and forefinger together as you draw the loop through and tighten up the knot.

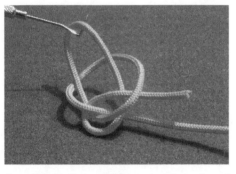

(the dental tool is being used here in place of my fingers because they look like sausages)

5. As the knot tightens, you can fine tune the size of the loop by pulling a bit on the tag end. Tighten the knot by pulling on the tag end and the loop. Finally, clip off excess tag end close to the knot.

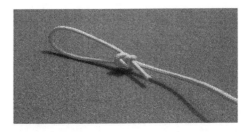

A small perfection loop is better than a big one, so try and keep your loop size to ½" or less in diameter. Again, practice will produce improved perfection loops very quickly.

Connecting Tippet to Leader with a Loop-to-Loop Connection

This assumes you've learned how to tie a Perfection Loop so that your tippet and your leader both have these loops on their respective ends. Connecting them using a loop-to-loop is very simple:

1. Pass the loop on the end of your new tippet section through the loop on the end of the leader.

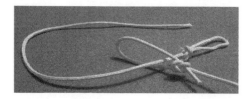

2. Pass the tag end of your tippet through the loop on the tippet.

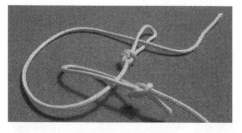

3. Pull on the tag end of the tippet until both loops link together. Voila—you did it!

The Art of the Cast

"It is an art that is performed on a four-count rhythm
between ten o'clock and two o'clock."

– A River Runs Through It

The cast is the centerpiece of fly fishing. Even for those
who have never lifted a fly rod or waded in a river, when
hearing the mention of fly fishing, it's the cast that comes
to mind. It embodies grace, power, gentleness and solitude. Little else in our lives can accomplish this wonderful blend of good karma. A lofty goal for sure, and in the
process you will surely founder a bit before your casting
technique achieves a modicum of those traits. But have
faith—it will come.

Norman Maclean wrote that "a*ll good things—trout as
well as eternal salvation—come by grace and grace comes*

by art and art does not come easy." He was talking about learning to fly cast, and it is sage advice to heed.

Let's get some basics down right up front. First, fly casting is not a strength game. Neither is it a distance contest. Finally, it's not a competitive sport, it's a *pastime*. Relax. Enjoy.

If you're a golfer, swinging a club has many parallels to casting a line. It's not how hard you swing, it's how smoothly your shoulders, elbows and wrists work together to hit the ball consistently. Think of Freddy Couples' swing—smoother than butter, unhurried and graceful. His arms don't bulge with muscles but they work with the wrists to produce a precision swing and long drives that all golfers envy.

So it is with casting a fly, but the golf analogy fades there. The three joints in your arm that matter in your cast are—in order of importance—the *wrist*, the *elbow* and the *shoulder*. Nothing else has any relevance in the cast.

While there is a school of thought that says one should keep the wrist fixed when casting, it is this writer's humble opinion that those folks are ~~nuts dead wrong~~ offering incorrect advice.

The wrist is most important because it controls the rod's position and is the best joint to impart speed to the rod. The elbow serves to help the wrist by adding speed to the arm to which the wrist is attached and thus adding speed to the rod. Finally, the shoulder will occasionally be called in to assist the wrist and elbow for some extra speed and thus distance when a really long cast is called for.

The wrist is pre-eminent among these joints—you can easily cast using it alone. In fact, you could spend a whole season fly fishing using only your wrist and your casts would be long enough to reach about 80% of the fish that a wrist-elbow-shoulder cast could target.

Which fits quite nicely into the *grace* element of the cast—the less movement, muscle and energy one puts into the cast, the more of an art it becomes. And art becomes grace, and grace feels very nice when it slides into your hand and up your arm and into your being.

With that in mind, let's move on to the mechanical process of casting a fly. (*Note to lefties:* these instructions assume right-handedness. Simply reverse the instructions for left-handed casting and you'll do fine).

I strongly suggest that you first read this in the quiet of your home, sitting in a comfortable chair with good light. Feel free to include an adult beverage. Take your first practice lesson in your mind. Get the cerebral feel of the rod in your hand as your wrist and arm begin casting without actually doing it. You can continue practicing like this anytime your mind tends to wander—sitting at the office, in church or at your kid's soccer game.

You'll find this mental exercise—I call it cybercasting—will make your first day outside with a rod in your hand much more rewarding with a much quicker learning curve.

Before you pick up your rod for your first real practice, let's look at how to hold the rod in your hand. It's pretty simple—the rod has a cork grip in front of the reel which should fit your hand nicely. Pick it up by the cork like you'd pick up a stick.

The only real option here is what to do with your thumb. If you have a strong wrist and grip, you can let it rest naturally along the left side of the handle. If you feel your wrist or your grip's strength could use some help— or if you just like the feel of it—put your thumb *on top* of the cork handle. Your thumb can now work as a lever to help your wrist stop your back cast quickly, and also to help put power into the rod on your forward cast.

We're going to cover the two basic casts that cover 99% of the casting situations you'll ever come across. These are 1) the *overhead cast* and 2) the *roll cast.* You may have already read articles expounding on all the special casting techniques needed for various situations, but these are almost always simply variations of these two basic casts. Master them and the odds are you will never need more.

So, with the rod comfortably in your hand, it's time to start the casting lesson.

The overhead cast: This is the classic cast we all see in our minds when we think of fly fishing—the long graceful back cast followed by the line shooting forward in a tight loop, coming to rest gently on the water. Almost all the other kinds of casts you may hear about are simply variations off this basic technique. So—learn this first!

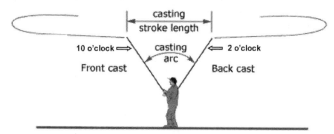

Using whichever grip you prefer, start with the rod in the right hand pointing forward and slightly downward so the tip is a foot or so off the water with 10-15' of fly line off the end of the rod in the water in front of you. In your left hand, hold the line coming off the reel so there is about 3' of line between your hand and the first eyelet on the rod. The left hand will be controlling the line while the right hand controls the rod.

Fly casting instruction always begins with this this mental image: you are a clock and the rod is the hour hand. With your rod sticking straight up, it's pointing at high noon. Stick your rod straight out in front of you and it's pointing to 9 o'clock. Point it behind you and it's at 3 o'clock. Your feet are at 6 o'clock (obviously, pointing your rod in this direction is a bad idea). Keep this in mind as you begin because it's in important concept.

With that in mind, let's begin. Using primarily your wrist but with some help from your elbow, lift the rod tip quickly up and backward, lifting the line off the water (or lawn) and into the air. Continue moving the rod backward past midday and into early afternoon, at which point abruptly halt your arm movement no later than 2 o'clock. Done properly, the line will be shooting past your rod tip and heading out behind you.

A critical point—the rod should move quickly enough to put a bend in it as it lifts the line off the water and sends it behind you. "Quickly" is the operative word for how you start and end the movement of the rod in either direction. It is that quickness that bends the rod at the beginning and stops the rod at the end.

Using the rod's flex is essential to a good cast. When you stop your wrist and arm as the rod approaches 2 o'clock, the rod will straighten out its bend and add energy to the line heading out behind you. If that happens, you are doing fine.

Here's a bit of fine tuning—if you hear your rod whistling through the air, you're moving it a wee bit too quickly. This is better than not going quickly enough, but you'll be wasting power and effort—and it's just not considered good style.

As the line moves behind you, hold the rod steady at 2 o'clock for about a half beat to give the line time to nearly straighten out behind you (but not so long that gravity takes over and the line falls to earth). After that momentary pause, reverse the process using your wrist and elbow to quickly move the rod forward towards mid-morning. Again, you should put enough speed into the rod to bend it as it tugs the line back towards the front.

At this point, if the line appears to be heading to its desired destination, just hold the rod at 10 o'clock and let the line shoot forward until it fully straightens out. As gravity drops it onto the water (or lawn), gently lower the rod to keep pointing at your line as it descends to the water. Done properly, your cast becomes a thing of grace. Not bad, huh?

Usually, though, it's not quite that simple. You may start with 15' of line hanging out of the rod, but the trout you're aiming at will be 25' away. You have a few options. You could pull another 10' of fly line off the reel ('stripping' in fly fishing parlance) before you begin your cast, letting it lie at your feet. Then do as described above, but add a few extra backwards-then-forwards casts (called "false casts") while your left hand lets the extra line feed into each false cast until your fly closes in on to the target. When it looks about right, complete your cast just as you did above so the fly line settles gently onto the water with your rod initially stopping at 10oclock, then descending with the line to end up parallel with the water at 9 o'clock.

Another option would be, rather than stripping the line off the reel before you begin casting, to strip a few feet of line off the reel with your left hand during each false cast, feeding it to the rod until it appears to be the proper length, then stopping the cast so the line and fly land gently on the water.

This requires a bit of practice, as it's the fly casting version of rubbing your stomach with one hand while tapping the top of your head with the other. We can all do that now but most of us needed a few tries to get it down. Same with casting.

Done properly, the fly will land 25' out and the trout will gobble it down. But with the inevitable mistakes and errors cooked into those early casts, the line will either go too far, not far enough or in the wrong direction. That's okay—we all do it. Strip in some line with your left hand until you have a comfortable length of line on the water, then cast again and adjust to correct the previous error.

IMPORTANT: If you're following this image in your mind, you will realize that your left hand is used not only to let line out, it will also be pulling line in. It can strip in about 3' of line before you have to let go of the fly line in order to reach forward to grab it closer to the rod eyelet for the next pull.

To prevent line from slipping back up the eyelets when you briefly let go of it, the line should be hooked under your right fore or index finger when stripping. As your left hand releases the line to grab it anew, the finger on your right hand should press the line snug against the handle so control is maintained.

This sounds complicated, but actually it will quickly become a natural instinct for you.

THE LOOP The prettiest—and most important—part of the classic cast is that tight, gravity-defying loop formed by the line as it goes back and forth. The first half of the line comes off the rod tip parallel to the water while the other half of the line traveling in the opposite direction is also parallel and only a foot or so above the first half.

Compare that to the novice's cast. Their loops are much rounder, tracing figure-8's high in the sky and slapping the water at either end. This results in short casts, fly and line piling up in a mess on the water, and trout chuckling as they dart away.

While there are lengthy tomes already written on casting technique, making the perfect loop can be boiled down to one easily understood concept. Understand this and you will soon be throwing casts with a very acceptable loop. Here it is:

The shape of the loop is defined by the lowest point of the rod tip during the cast—the higher the tip remains, the tighter the loop becomes.

The bottom of the loop will be determined by the lowest point of your rod tip during the cast. The top of the loop will mirror the bottom of the loop. For example, if the lowest point of your tip during a cast is 4' lower than its highest point, the loop will about 8' wide from bottom to top, making a big figure-8 loop with little distance or accuracy—and it looks icky.

With a 10-to-2 rod movement, "tip dip" is minimized, reducing loop size while keeping the loop elevated which increases distance and accuracy. Instead of a figure-8 loop, you get a long and aesthetically pleasing narrow oval. That's when grace begins to emerge and piscatorial chuckling becomes a thing of the past.

When you see someone throwing a beautifully tight loop, set the envy aside for a moment and watch their rod tip. The best casters actually keep their rods moving closer to 11-to-1, producing very little tip dip and resulting in that artful, tight loop.

All beginners let their rods go way beyond 10 and 2—it appears built into our homo sapien DNA. The good news is our DNA also lets us learn new stuff, like keeping our rod between 10 and 2. It won't happen instantly, but the more you practice, the better you'll get.

In fact, after a half hour of casting with 'tip dip' in mind, you should be producing reasonably tight loops which will reward you with reasonably accurate casts and reasonably good results with the fish.

This is classic trial-and-error work. You will catch the willows behind you, snag the fly into your shirt sleeve, have the line, leader and fly tumble in a heap in front of you. But be assured that you'll be much better after

30 minutes of casting practice. And much better after another 30 minutes. And so on.

The roll cast: You will often find yourself in situations where the overhead cast can't be made, standing on a river bank with shrubs, willows, or a cliff directly behind you. This is where you use your roll cast, a simple cast that keeps your line always in front of you to avoid those obstacles behind you.

First, start with 10-15' of line past the rod tip and just flip it out in front of you as much as possible without taking it behind you.

With your rod facing 9 o'clock, slowly raise it up and a bit to the right until it's pointing just past vertical and slightly behind you—say, 11:30. The first 10' or so of line will be hanging straight down off your right shoulder with the rest of it in front of you on the water.

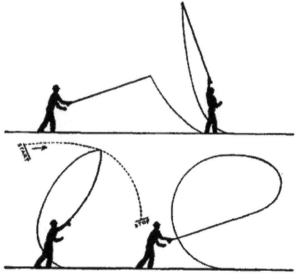

Hold the line with your left hand or by pressing it against the handle with your finger on the right hand just above the reel. Now 'punch' your right arm forward and at the same time flick your wrist down so the rod quickly goes to 10 o'clock.

That's all there is to the cast. Done properly, the line will loop up and out in front of you to its full length and land gently on the water. With practice, you'll be able to do this with 30' or more of line, which lets you avoid those willows directly behind you and reach your target under most situations.

You should practice both casting accuracy and casting distance, with the former being more important than the latter. On all but the very large rivers, you will rarely need to cast more than 60', and 40' will cover the vast majority of fish catching opportunities. However, an ill-placed fly will rarely catch anything, so focus on accuracy. Distance will come naturally as your technique improves.

It's best to do your first practice session away from water in an open area with nothing large in your way. A lawn, an athletic field or any open, grassy area are all great places to practice (avoid paved surfaces as they will quickly destroy the finish of your fly line). Also, don't put a fly on the end of the line—not only is it not necessary when practicing, you'll be ruining a perfectly good fly while putting friends, pets and yourself at needless risk of impalement.

Fly Line Management

..."if you have never picked up a fly rod before, you will soon find it factually and theologically true that man by nature is a damn mess."

— *A River Runs Through It*

Fly line management specifically refers to the line that is off the reel but not yet through the first eyelet on your rod. It can range from just a few feet to 20' of line or more, depending on the conditions.

Keeping this line organized while casting is probably the least practiced part of the whole fly fishing experience, but it's one you should plan to be at least reasonably good at doing. Otherwise, you'll spend too much of your day dealing with spaghetti-like tangles in the line lying at your feet, tripping over line wrapped around your ankle, and chasing your dog to get the line unwrapped from his neck. Even worse—and guaranteed this will happen at least once—you'll lose a big fish when it breaks off during a big run because you're standing on your line.

There are many ways to manage your fly line, but all involve your left hand. There is the classic eastern style of using your fingers to coil the line in neat little figure-8's held in the palm of the hand. This elegant technique works well on small New England babbling brooks, but it is quickly overpowered when fishing bigger, faster waters.

A more common approach when stripping in line is to hold loops of line in your left hand, each loop being 1-2' in diameter. As you make a new cast, these loops are released into the cast one or two loops at a time until you have the proper length of line in the air. This technique requires that you keep the loops laying side by side in your hand so they go back into the next cast in the reverse order that they came in from the previous cast. Done wrong, you will soon have a bowl of spaghetti on your hands or jammed in the eyelet of your rod.

Another approach, and for many the easiest way, is to simply let line fall at your feet as it's stripped in. The downside is that water currents like to drag it between your legs and around the closest log. You also can get it wrapped under your feet. It takes awareness and patience but only a minimum of coordination.

Whatever approach you take to keeping the line organized, patience and practice are the keys to success here.

CHAPTER 5

All About Insects

Basic Bug Stuff:
Latin-free Entomology

Let's assume you're not an entomologist. Good, because you don't need to be one. Entomologists know all the names for kingdom, phylum, class, order and species of insects in both English and Latin. Bully for them. We prefer names we can remember in our native tongue. With that, let us begin.

Fish love insects but they're really hard to put on a hook, thus the reason for the artificial fly. Each fly is designed to look sort of like a particular kind of insect. Some fly designs are highly intricate to be an exact replica of a specific insect. Others are made to look sort of like a broader range of critters—these are called generics. All work well under the right circumstances.

Insects found around waters fall into six general categories—Caddisflies, mayflies, stoneflies, midges, terrestrials and bugs-we-can't-identify. We'll focus on the first five groups here.

The first four groups are types of *aquatic insects*, spending almost their whole lives living on the bottom of rivers and streams, metamorphosing after 1-7 years to grow wings, fly, make babies, and die. The fifth group, *terrestrials*, includes insects and other edible creatures that live on land but accidentally fall in the water to become a fish snack.

The Hatch

Before we get into bug details, first understand how these little things live and die around the water, and how it impacts you as a fisherman.

When a particular species of aquatic insect hatches, all the mature members of that species seem to do it en masse at various times of day over a period of a few days to a few weeks, triggered by some mysterious combination of water temps, air temps, wind speed, sunlight and time of day. One moment all is quiet, the next there are insects all over the river, filling the air, floating on the surface and flying up your nose. This is called a *hatch*.

During a hatch, the insect is vulnerable to becoming part of a trout's meal. The hatch is actually a very brief but complex biological process that is the culmination of years of life below the surface. When that mysterious urge arrives, the last act of the insect in its nymphal form is to swim quickly from the stream bottom to the surface, where it struggles to get through the surface film while wriggling out of its nymphal shell to emerge as a newborn—and airborne—insect. Trout love this moment as these defenseless, almost immobile critters are some of the easiest snacks of the day.

While resting on the surface letting their wings dry, trout continue to eat them. Survivors finally take to the air where they get to meet and greet others of their kind, eventually deciding on a procreatable mate. Following a brief few moments of mid-air passion, the guy fly sputters and falls into the water dead to become a likely fish snack. The female lays her eggs on the water's surface a few at a time, dodging feeding fish until all her eggs are gone, which is just about the time her engine cuts out and she falls to earth for the last time to also become a likely fish snack.

There are many variants of this process—some species crawl up on the bank, a rock, or up into the willows to metamorphose into their flying state. Some prefer to die on land rather than water. But in general, they all follow this cycle.

Fish are unpredictable as to which insects in which stage of life will be the preferred *snack du moment.* You may find four different hatches underway at once with trout just feeding on one of them and only in their emerging state. An hour later, the insects may change and the trout's feeding preferences could be totally different. Understanding what is happening insect-wise at any point in time will help you pick out the fly in your collection with the best chance of success.

This is called *matching the hatch.* It would probably be more accurately called *trying* to match the hatch, because it can be a bit frustrating tying on one fly after another without success while the waters churn around you with feeding trout.

Some days a fly that is generally the right size and color is all you need. Other days, the most subtle difference in size or color can be the difference between being totally ignored and totally slammed. However, once you stumble upon the perfect fly, bad memories vanish and your surroundings are suddenly a magical day that makes any earlier frustration well worth the effort.

The Insects

Caddisflies: These are easily identified when they're airborne by their erratic, flitting flight patterns. When not flying, their wings lay either flat  or "tented" along the length of their body. They live for 1-3 years among the rocks and gravel on stream bottoms as nymphs before metamorphosing into their winged version. Once airborne, they live for only a few days to a few weeks.

Mayflies: These are the ballerinas of aquatic insects, with a gentle flight pattern. When not flying, their wings  are held upright like a butterfly. After 1-2 years grubbing around the bottom of their waters, they emerge and are ready to mate. The males gently rise up and down over the water in a graceful dance, grab a willing mate out of the air, introduce themselves, make a bunch of babies, then drop dead on the water and then fish eat them. Not a great life.

The females are not so lucky. Before they die, they have to drop their eggs a few at a time onto the water's surface while dodging hungry fish. Then they die and fish eat them.

Stoneflies: These are the freight helicopters of the aquatic insect world. They have two pairs of wings, and fly slow, steady, and straight. Their wings, when not fly-ing, lay flat but don't "tent" like caddisflies. Stoneflies typically live 1-3 years on the stream bottoms (with a few making it 7 years!) before emerging onto rocks and streamside foliage to change into their winged versions.

While some are quite small, some stoneflies can be sev-eral inches long, making them a fish favorite.

Midges: These are small aquatic insects, usually so small that they are tough to identify. When you look along the edge of a river or

lake, you often see swarms of tiny little bugs scurrying on the surface. These are midges. Their entire life cycle is measured in weeks, so there are always midges in every life stage present in the water all the time. trout eat them constantly, but because of their small size, it can be tough to find any fly to fool them. Best bet is go with tiny wire-like nymph patterns simulating the pre-flight midge lar-vae. Definitely bring your magnifiers to tie these little buggers on.

Terrestrials: Born on land but living near the water, terrestrials are an important food source for trout because they are often big (grasshoppers), tasty (worms, nightcrawlers), and sometimes numerous (ants). trout love to gobble terrestrials, and since they only arrive by accident, trout seem willing to grab them even when they're ignoring aquatic insects.

You should always have some flies patterned after the local terrestrial population, be it grasshoppers, beetles, ants, or worms.

Anatomy of an Artificial Fly

Understanding the components of an artificial fly will help you understand how it works, which will help you select the proper fly to deal with whatever circumstances you find yourself facing on the water. It will also help understand other fishermen when they start rambling on about hackle, dubbing, wing material and thorax size.

First, the hook. Hooks come in various sizes and shapes. For the average trout fisherman, the shape varies little, making size the only important vari-

able. While no official size classification standard exists, manufacturers follow a common naming convention of assigning numbers to hook sizes. The bigger the number, the smaller the hook.

The sizes shown here will cover 95% of flies you'll be using your first year or two, and most of that will be using flies between 12 and 16.

The hook is made up of several parts:

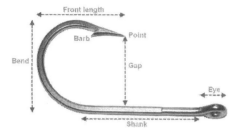

Almost all flies are tied to the shank, with some nymph patterns extending down to include the first part of the bend. Whether it's a dry fly, nymph or streamer, flies are made up of most if not all of these basic components—hackle, body (also called the thorax), wing, head and tail.

Here is a classic stonefly dry fly imitation, a Stimulator which shows all the standard components:

Dry flies: Dry flies are intended to float, so they use light materials that help the fly rest upon the surface. The wire used in a dry fly hook is relatively thin, the materials making up the body selected for their floatability.

Elk and deer hair are popular materials here because the hairs are hollow and tend to bob like a cork. The dry fly body is often made of fluffy, wooly material that can hold air bubbles within it. Some dries use hackle wrapped around the body to hold the fly off the surface.

Here's a classic dry fly pattern, the elk hair caddis. It doesn't have a head or a tail but has all the other components.

Palmered hackle

Notice the hair-like wrapping on the body. This is called palmered hackle and provides a thicker body profile without adding weight. It also helps keep the fly afloat on top of the water.

Most caddis dry fly patterns don't have a tail, while most mayfly dries do.

Nymphs: Nymphs are frequently tied with added weight, historically lead or copper wire wrapped around the shank before the other materials are applied. In the past few decades, a very popular alternative approach is to add a brass bead or two at the fly's head. This provides weight to help drop the fly near the bottom, and also adds a bit of attention-getting flash.

Bead head

Here is an example of a nymph, another classic pattern using a bead head—the prince nymph. The two flat white wings are what distinguish a prince nymph from similar patterns, and are made of biots, the small, stiff barbs from the feather found on the leading edge of large bird wings (e.g., goose, turkey).

My favorite fly pattern name was given to a modified prince nymph tied by a friend who used phosphorescent Mylar strips in place of the biots. He called it "The Nymph Formerly Known As Prince."

Emergers: Emergers are an interesting class of artificial flies, a hybrid of dry and nymph patterns that simulate aquatic insects as they are changing from their nymphal state to their airborne mode. During this transition, the nymph quickly swims to the water's surface to begin struggling out of its nymphal case as it sits suspended in the surface film of the water. Its head is emerging of the water and its body is beneath the surface. It is a favorite time for trout to gobble bugs, as the emerger is completely defenseless.

These patterns combine elements of nymphs and dry flies, with the front of the fly floating and the rear of the fly hanging below the surface.

Here's a good example that includes deer hair hackle at the front and mostly on top of the fly,

with a slim body with just a minimal wrap to promote sinking below the surface, and no tail.

When fishing these, only apply floatant to the head of the fly so the tail end has no difficulty slipping below the surface film.

Streamers: Streamers imitate small, bite-sized fish that bigger fish consume when given the chance. As such, they are normally the biggest flies in your kit. They tend to have full bodies and long tails tied with soft materials that easily wave in the current as they are retrieved through the water. Since they imitate fish, weight is often added to the shank to help move the fly down into the water column. Some streamers get big and heavy enough that casting them is more of an overhand lob than a delicate cast. However, since big fish like to eat big bait, the rewards can be well worth a bit of cumbersome casting.

Wet flies: Wet flies imitate swimming insects, typically a nymph quickly heading to the surface to begin metamorphosis. They are typically tied with a collar of relatively long, soft hackles that "swim" with a pulsating movement when swept through the water, simulating the nymphal legs that propel the little guys to the surface.

Many of these patterns have been around since Isaak Walton misspelled "Compleat." Despite being long in the tooth, they still can be some of the most productive flies in your collection. Always keep a few of these in reserve for those days when nothing else seems to be working.

Presenting the Fly

Dry Flies

"He told us about Christ's disciples being fishermen,
and we were left to assume, as my brother and I did,
that all first-class fishermen on the Sea of Galilee were
fly fishermen, and John, the favorite, was a dry-fly
fisherman."

— *A River Runs Through It*

Dry flies imitate insects that are sitting on the surface of
the water. This makes them easy prey to a fish, and when

a trout eats one, you see it happen. Not only does it make for exciting "target" casting to a feeding fish, you also get to watch it take your fly. Sometimes it's a splashy aggressive take, other times it might be a gentle sip. Whichever way it happens, to a fly fisherman there's nothing more exciting than catching fish on a dry fly.

Because dry flies sit on the top of the water, their movement is at the whim of the currents on the surface. To imitate such a bug, an artificial fly should float freely like a real insect and not be dragged unnaturally by the current pulling on the leader. Remember that, with few exceptions, surface-resting insects don't swim so any fly not floating naturally with the current will be suspect to a fish.

You can minimize drag on your fly by shaping your cast so there is an upstream 'belly' in your line between your fly and your rod. This minimizes the current's influence on the fly, allowing it to drift naturally.

If you can't get the belly in the line with the cast, you can put one in once the line lands on the water by 'mending'. Mending is simply flipping a belly of line upstream with your rod. A properly mended line will put belly in the line without pulling on the fly. A gentle upstream flip of the rod tip with some extra line works best, but this is another example of "practice makes perfect."

Nymphs

Nymphs are the first stage of life for aquatic insects. While at first glance all nymphs look alike, there are subtle differences between caddis, mayfly, and stonefly nymphs. Some have 3 tail stems, some have 2. Some have gills on their sides, some underneath. Some are chubby and others slender. You can study these subtle differences if you wish, but trout don't really seem to care if your fly has a moderately incorrect number of tail whiskers. If your fly is generally the size and color that they're currently eating, it has a good chance to draw the curiosity of a trout.

Fishing with nymphs makes sense, particularly when fishing for trout—about 80% of a trout's diet is made up of nymphs. It's pretty common for nymph fishermen to out-catch dry fly fishermen consistently day after day (dry fly fishermen will blaspheme me for revealing that secret).

The key to nymph fishing is to get your fly down near the bottom and then to let it drift naturally for as long as possible. Fish are looking for nymphs that have become dislodged from rocks and gravel and are floating just off the bottom. The more natural the drift, the better the odds of getting a fish to bite.

To get the fly near the bottom requires weight. One method is to use a sinking line, but who really wants to change fly lines back and forth as feeding preferences change? Nope, that just ain't a good option, which leaves you with using weighted flies and/or adding weight to your leader.

Many nymphs these days are tied with a brass or copper bead (or two) at the head, adding weight and making it easier to get to the bottom. These work well but in deeper and/or faster water, you may still need to add weight by putting a split shot or two on the line a foot or so up from the fly.

Now that it's down near the bottom, you've lost the visual advantage of dry fly fishing in that you no longer see the fish taking your fly. If you don't know it's taken your fly, you won't catch the fish.

To solve this problem, the fly fishing industry came up with a device similar to the red and white bobbers used by cane pole fishermen, usually tied a few feet above a glob of nightcrawlers. Being much more sophisticated than mere cane pole fishermen, the fly fishing industry couldn't admit to using bobbers so they relabeled it with the much more sophisticated moniker *strike indicator*.

These come in several styles, from a tuft of wool or poly tied to the leader to tiny little red and white pieces of cork (yes, just like a bobber). Whichever you use, you know a trout has taken your nymph when the ~~bobber~~ *strike indicator* gets pulled underwater.

Wet Flies and Streamers

Streamers are designed to imitate swimming non-insect critters like small fish and leaches. They come in all colors, shapes and sizes, but have the common traits of a bit of weight built into the fly to sink it into the water column and long feathers or fur strips to give it a fish-like body and movement.

Wet flies simulate swimming insects, typically those that are struggling madly to get from their bottom-crawling nymphal condition up to the suface where they hope to get airborne and go on their first—and last—date. Wet flies are smaller than streamers, may have a tiny bit of added weight to keep them subsurface, and have some soft, flexible hackle feathers that simulate the pulsation of swimming nymphal legs.

Wet flies and streamers are used in a similar fashion. Typically they are cast across the current or slightly up-current, then swept through and across the current. Your chances of attracting a fish's attention will be greatly enhanced by imparting a swimming motion to the fly by gently wiggling or jiggling the rod tip as the fly moves through the water. This creates a bit of movement in the softer parts of the fly and looks more life-like to your target.

Unlike nymph fishing, when a fish decides your streamer or wet fly is edible, that decision will definitely *not* go unnoticed. By always having pressure on the line while the fly moves through the water, you feel the fish strike instantly, like a jolt of electricity up your arm and into your spine. This is a very fun way to fish!

CHAPTER 6

Getting to the fish

Row v. Wade

"One great thing about fly fishing is that after a while nothing exists of the world but thoughts of fly fishing."

– A River Runs Through It

FISH LIVE IN WATER, AND WE HAVE TWO WAYS TO approach them—on foot or in a boat. Neither has a functional or spiritual advantage over the other. Some people prefer to float, some prefer to wade, and most will do whichever is available at the moment.

Wade

Wade fishing has some significant advantages. First, convenience clearly belongs in the wader's corner. If you decide to go fishing, preparation time is limited to how long it takes to throw your gear into the back of your car. Once you arrive at the water, you can be taking your first cast almost immediately.

Second, once positioned in your selected stretch of water, you can "work the pool," leisurely trying its every little nook and cranny in search of trout. While at first glance a stretch of water may yield one or two obvious holding spots for trout, most have many more subtle places where trout may be, and more importantly places where other fishermen may have overlooked.

Stepping into a boulder-strewn section of water can provide enough opportunities to keep you engaged for hours without wearing out your welcome with its inhabitants. Trying different spots with different flies delivered with different casts all within a span of a few dozen yards is not only enjoyable, it becomes a self-teaching classroom for gathering advanced fly fishing knowledge that no book learning can hope to achieve.

Third, wading gives you mobility. You can move upstream or downstream at your own pace. You can drive to another stretch of water or to another stream if things get slow.

And finally, the moment you realize you've had your fill of fishing for the day, you can simply pack your stuff up and head home or to the local watering hole to debrief the day with whoever occupies the bar stool next to you.

Row

Fly fishing from a boat—the iconic image that comes to mind is two guys in a raft or drift boat with a guide. It is still probably the most common float fishing approach taken, but these days you have many alternative options for watercraft designed for fishing.

Float tubes, catarafts, canoes, kayaks, and paddle boards all come with fishing-focused options including rod holders and anchor systems. But for the novice fly fisherman, the desire to use one of these should be held in check till next season. For this discussion, let's focus on the traditional two-guys-in-a-boat-with-a-guide approach.

What are the advantages to this approach? One big plus is the guide, who knows how to drive the boat, knows the waters and the most productive holes, and is full of good advice. The guide helps you select the right fly, tells you where to put it, and is typically filled with a plethora of anecdotal information that will help flesh out your fly fishing knowledge and learn a few new jokes (NOTE: if you like your guide enough to use him again, expect to hear the same jokes next time).

Like most pastimes, fly fishing expertise comes by a combination of mastering a few mechanical processes (e.g., casting) coupled with a continually growing array of small, anecdotal pieces of information. A good guide will load you up with an ample supply of valuable anecdotes, some of which have nothing to do with fishing but are fun to hear nonetheless.

For some reason, being a successful guide requires being both a fisherman and a storyteller. Most of them are good at both, and it always makes for a memorable day.

Another advantage to floating is that you can cover a much greater amount of water than you can wading. A typical day's float trip may cover 6-12 miles of water, usually at a leisurely pace. You will not only have a wide variety of fishing conditions, it offers the opportunity to observe the broader watershed's beauty as you quietly drift through it. This is your chance to see how the birds, wildlife, geological formations, forests, shrubs and wildflowers all play a role in making the river experience a much greater experience than just having a neat place to fish.

Another plus with floating is that you do most of your fishing with short casts. It is a rare moment when you'd need to make more than a 30' cast, and most casts would be more in the 20-30' range. Short casts means more accurate casts, and that means more success in hooking up fish.

So what's the down side? First, spontaneity is lost. You normally can't suddenly decide to do it and order up a guide for the day. Float trips take some advance planning to reserve a guide, select the waters to be floated, make travel arrangements, find a partner, etc. When your float day arrives, you are basically stuck with whatever weather conditions Mother Nature whips up. Rain, wind, cold—you pretty much have deal with it.

Secondly, guides are not free. A guide and boat for the day can easily run beyond $500, and don't forget that guides live for tips. Be kind.

Third, while you will cover lots of water, you don't get to linger over every good looking hole to learn its nuances. Your guide knows how much time it will take to make the float and he will keep the boat moving along so you reach the takeout on schedule.

So, for the decision of row v. wade—there is no right choice. They are both fun ways to go fishing. You'll probably find you like doing both, and the flexibility of your schedule and the thickness of your wallet will determine the frequency of each.

You Have a Fish on the Line – Now What?

Finally, after all that reading, spending money on gear, practice, frustration and disappointment—you hook yourself a fish on a fly!

Congratulations in advance, because you will remember that moment for the rest of your life. Whether that memory is of the ache that comes with losing the fish before you get to hold it in your hands, or of the excitement captured in a photo of you holding it up with a beaming grin depends on how well you study this section. Plus some luck of course.

The Setup

Let's start with what you should be doing when your fly is on the water, drifting toward the spot where you've seen a rising trout sipping bugs off the surface:

- *Keep your eyes glued to your fly.* You rarely feel a fish taking a dry fly—you have to see it to know it's happened. This is what makes dry fly fishing so exciting—you have the buildup of anticipation culminated with a sudden, splashy visual reward. [NOTE: If you lose sight of your fly, just watch the area where you think it is. If you see a trout rise, assume it's eating your fly.]

- *Take excess slack out of your line* by stripping it in with your left hand so that there is 2-3' extra line between you and the fly. Too much slack and you'll not be able to set the hook quickly, leaving you with nothing but a fly on the end of your line and a four-letter frown in your brain.

- *Repeat.* If the fly floats past the fish with no results, let it drift 5-6' past, then recast 5-6' above its feeding point and try it again. It could take a half dozen drifts past it before it decides to investigate your offering.

  Each trout has its own feeding rhythm. One might eat a fly every 10 seconds while his next door neighbor might grab one every two minutes. Watch for that rhythm and time your cast to put your fly over it when it's ready to eat again.

The Take

In a reasonably perfect world, the trout will eventually take your fly. It may be a splashy smash, it may be a slow porpoise-like roll or it could be a barely noticeable sip.

When you see the "take," you have to set the hook quickly. Fish have spent their whole lives eating bugs and know what a real one feels like. Your fly won't feel like a real insect, and the fish will very quickly sense it's a fake and immediately spit it out with a twitch of its gills.

It's between the initial take and that gill twitch—less than a second—when you need to "set the hook" by pulling up and back with your rod tip. It shouldn't be a violent yank—that will almost always break your tippet and you'll be out a fly as well as a fish. A quick lifting up of the rod tip coupled with a pull on the line with your left hand to help take up slack is usually sufficient to deliver enough of a yank to slip the hook into the fish's lip.

Be forewarned—the odds are that you'll be a bit late or a bit early when setting the hook the first few times a trout hits your fly. It's a normal part of mastering the art to make a few goofy misses before your eye, arm and wrist start working together to get that critical timing down.

The Fight

Fish don't like getting caught. They will swim hard to get away, they'll jump, they'll dive under logs and brush, they'll rub their lip in the gravel and on rocks. Any one of these maneuvers can easily dislodge the hook. To prevent that, you need to always have a steady pressure on the fish so the hook stays embedded and the fish stays away from logs, brush, gravel and rocks.

In the old days before the catch-and-release ethic took hold, playing the fish until it was exhausted was a time-honored approach to bringing the fish to net. Unfortunately, the more energy expended fighting against the fisherman, the less chance of it living when released. In those old days, it was normally "released" into a wicker creel hanging off one's hip, putting its survival odds at zero. Exhausting a fish that was going to die anyway didn't really make much difference.

These days, we've grown to like the idea of returning caught fish to the water to give it the chance to live to fight another day. To insure it lives, it's important to leave it with enough spare energy to survive after it's caught.

This means you don't let it flounder about or let it make run after run until it weakly swims up to your feet. Keep the pressure up without horsing it in (that's bad style too) so that the fish still has plenty of spunk left after it's in your net or in your hand.

Pressure should be steady but not punishing. Your tippet may only be able to handle a pull of 2-4 pounds, which even a small fish can produce under the right circumstances. Should a fish put on a strong surge as it tries to swim away, let it take line by letting it slip through your left hand's fingers while maintaining pressure on the fish.

The flex in your rod is critical to playing a fish successfully. Sudden jerks and pulls by the fish are absorbed by the rod so the tippet stays intact. To take full advantage of its flex, keep your rod tip pointing up during the fight, keeping it positioned between 10 o'clock and noon.

Be very careful not to take the rod past noon, as the further into the afternoon you go, the better the chance of over-bending your rod's tip and shattering it into little shards of graphite interspersed with very bad words coming out of your mouth.

There are two equally valid schools of thought on the role your reel plays when fighting a fish. One school says the reel has no role, and instead line should be retrieved by your left hand as the fish eventually tires, slows down and comes to you. This requires that technique explained earlier, using a finger on your right hand to keep the line tight while your left hand strips. Should the fish take a strong run, let line slip back to maintain steady but not excess pressure.

The other school says to use the reel to control your line. Typically, this involves reeling up excess line with your left hand while your right finger keeps control and pressure on the line (and the fish). Once the excess line is on the reel, it can be used to maintain pressure while reeling in line as the fish slows down.

If you have a fly reel that includes an adjustable drag, the second school is for you. A reel's drag system lets you adjust how hard it is to pull line off the reel. If you're catching big fish with a strong tippet, you might want to have your drag cranked up. Fir smaller fish and light tippet, you may crank it way back to little or no resistance. By adjusting the amount of drag to fit the conditions (fish size, tippet strength), your reel can provide much of the necessary pressure and cushioning of the fish's surges, increasing the odds of landing your prey.

Most drag adjustments are a simple knob on the side of the reel, designed to let you adjust it easily while in mid-fight.

The Landing

There are two basic ways to capture the fish—with a net or with your hand. Again, there is no right or wrong, it's all personal preference.

Using a net: Using a net is the easiest way, and done properly it won't harm the fish in any way. The key to a smooth net capture is to bring the fish to the net rather than swiping at the fish with the net.

First, don't bother picking up your net until the fish is close and your left hand is no longer involved in retrieving line. Once the fish is close, hold the net in your left hand and place it in the water with its far edge submerged about 6." Now use the rod to lift the fish toward the surface and lead him over the net. As it slips over the front of the net so its body is over the middle of the net, simply lift the net out of the water and the fish will be in it.

Lift the fish out of the water as little as possible. Its gills only work underwater, so it can run out of oxygen quickly once out of the water. The gills can also dry quickly which can be a fatal injury. It's best to leave the net partly submerged so the fish is underwater but still in the net while you remove your hook.

Photo ops should be done quickly so its airborne time is minimized. When you take your photo, hold the fish

with a hand on its tail and the other under its belly—
don't hold it up by the gills or the jaw! Just keep in mind
how you'd prefer to be held up for a pic—not by the lip
or the ears for sure.

Using your hand: If you don't use a net, your hand can
do the trick for you, but there is more opportunity to
injure the fish if not done correctly.

First, just like the technique used with a net, bring the
fish to your hand rather than trying to grab the fish with
your hand. Also, never handle the fish without first wet-
ting your hands—that protects the fish's protective slime.

Holding your hand open with the palm up and slightly
submerged, slide the fish over your palm, then lift the fish
up so it's laying squarely across the palm of your hand.

Resist the urge to grasp the fish with your fingers! That
may seem counter-intuitive, but it works. For some reason, fish are not inherently afraid when feeling pressure
from beneath them, which is what you're doing when
you lift it out of the water with an open hand. However,
closing fingers around them is cause for an instant fish
freak-out, and your instinct will then be to grip it harder
to hold on as it thrashes. That not only can easily crush
its internal organs, it will remove the protective slime on
its body which sets it up for a fungal infection not long
after its release. It also simply doesn't work very well—the
fish will usually slip right out of your hand and back in
the water, sometimes leaving your fly embedded in your
thumb as a going-away present.

Once out of the water and resting quietly on your
hand, gently remove the hook and set the fish gently back
in the water.

A variation of a hand-based landing is doing a *touch-less landing*. This only works if the fly is clearly visible in its lip, which happens most of the time. As the fish comes to your left hand, use your thumb and forefinger to grasp the fly by it shank. The eyelet will be pointing up towards your rod tip. Once you have a firm grip, lift the fish partly out of the water by the fly, then quickly rotate the fly 180 degrees so the eyelet is pointing down. A quick shake of the fly lets the fish's weight pull itself off the hook to drop harmlessly back into the water without ever being touched.

Granted, you don't get a photo op this way, but the mental image of that beautiful fish will stay with you forever.

Regardless of your hook removal technique, it is always best to be done with barbless or crimped-barb hooks. These rarely injure the fish, and hook removal is always easy.

Releasing the Fish

Much is made about holding your about-to-be-released catch steady in the current, moving its tail back and forth to simulate swimming in an effort to restore its strength.

That is really not necessary. What you want to insure is that it has enough strength to swim off on its own power. Without that strength, the fish will be powerless to avoid injury as the current bashes it against the rocks as it drifts downstream.

To prevent this, hold the fish with either hand placed under its belly so it is upright and facing upstream. It will know when it's ready to swim away. You don't have to wiggle its tail or shove it back and forth—most of the time it will blast away immediately, only rarely will it linger for a minute or so till it regains its breath.

Patience is the key here. If you have to wait a minute for it to revive, just enjoy looking at the beautiful fish you just caught that you're letting free. It's always a nice moment.

CHAPTER 7

Fly Fishing Etiquette

THERE ARE A FEW SPECIFIC RULES AND A FEW GENERAL rules of thumb covering basic behavior while fly fishing. Most are fairly obvious, but just so you can't use obliviousness as an excuse for bad behavior, here are some of the important ones:

Obvious Rules

1. Don't act like a jerk. Nobody likes that. Relax. Be nice.

2. Be forgiving. Don't let jerks ruin your day. They're probably just being oblivious, not purposefully obnoxious.

3. Be considerate. If you do run into a purposefully obnoxious person, hide their body in the bushes well above the ordinary high water line.

Less Obvious Rules

1. Know the local private property laws—What is legal access in one state may considered trespassing in another. For example, Colorado law lets a private landowner own the river bottom and keep you from wading it (in fact, while you could float that water, you would not be allowed to drop anchor!) Go north a few hundred miles to Montana and the

public is guaranteed use of all waters as long as you stay below the ordinary high water mark.

2. If you're not sure of local regulations, ask at a local fly shop to get those details. They know everything.

3. Ask permission. If you have to cross what appears to be private property to reach the water, go knock on their door and politely ask permission. Not doing that is acting like a jerk. See above.

4. Don't crowd your fellow fisherman. Granted, "crowding" is a relative term depending on the waters you're fishing. If it's opening day of trout season in New Jersey, you may find yourself shoulder-to-shoulder with many others, while in the Rockies you may be the only person in sight for hours at a time. Use common sense—be polite. Don't cast into another fisherman's casting area and don't wade through the water they're fishing.

5. If fishing uncrowded waters, try to stay out of sight of others if possible. If someone is fishing a pool when you arrive, quietly make your way up or downstream far enough so that you both have your own water and sight lines to yourselves.

6. A wading fisherman has the right of way over boats. If you're in a boat, if possible avoid floating through the wader's target water (pass behind, pull to the far shore, etc.) If conditions offer multiple options, ask the wader which route they'd prefer you to take as you approach.

7. Despite this rule, if you're wading, keep a wary eye on approaching boats. One of them may have a

jerk at the helm who doesn't know the rules, and being knocked flat by a raft can ruin your day.

8. Don't litter. Keep a pocket set aside for trash. This includes old tippets as well as paper and coffee lids. Follow the adage "take nothing but pictures, leave nothing but footprints."

9. Respect gates. If you come across a gate while crossing land to reach water, remember the rule—"if it's open, leave it open; if it's closed, close it behind you."

10. Be quiet. Sure, hoot if you must when you hook up a pig, but generally let nature be the dominant sound maker. Fly fishing is not simply about catching fish, it is about finding solitude, becoming sensitive to those beautiful surroundings. Nothing ruins that more than a loud, boisterous insensitive boor with a fly rod in their hand. If you act like that, your body may end up hidden in the bushes well above the ordinary high water line.

CHAPTER 8

Fly tying

"Nobody has put in a good day's fishing unless he leaves
a couple of flies hanging in the bushes. You can't catch
fish if you don't dare go where they are."

– A River Runs Through It

TYING FLIES IS A REWARDING PASTIME. THERE IS NOTH-
ing quite like making a fly out of a mat of hair you
clipped off your dog and then go out and catch a trout
with it.

That's the good news. Here's reality—you're going to
spend hundreds of dollars on a tying bench, vise, hackle,
assorted feathers and furs, threads, bobbins, bodkins,

hair stackers, scissors, hackle pliers, hooks, glue, resin, dubbing needles, whip finishers and a few dozen other doodads you've never heard of. Then you need to buy a bunch of books or take a class to learn how to use all those things. Next you have to find a place in the house for your fly tying nook that passes your spouse's muster. And when it's all in place, you might find that you just suck at fly tying.

So here's my recommendation—wait a while. Buy your flies from the local fly shop for your first year or so. Find out if you're going to like fly fishing for the rest of your life, or only until golf season starts. If and when you realize you're hooked for life, give fly tying a try. It is a wonderful hobby for those cold winter days when you can't fish but want to be immersed in the concept anyway.

And once you start tying, you'll tell your spouse you're saving money by not buying as many flies. Which of course is a complete lie because you'll still go to the fly shop and spend that money on another doodad, but it somehow helps justify the whole process.

Hey, whatever it takes.

CHAPTER 9

Conclusion

"I am haunted by waters."

– A River Runs Through It

IF YOU'VE REACHED THIS POINT IN THE BOOK, IT'S SAFE to assume you will be giving fly fishing a tryout. In that case, this book has succeeded in achieving its basic goal.

Hopefully these lessons will help you to master the basic mechanics of fly fishing. More importantly, they also provide you with the opportunity to understand and appreciate the aesthetics, the ethic and the solitude of fly fishing that fit in so naturally with those mechanics. Together they form a much greater whole than the sum of their parts.

So now it's time to go out, spend a few bucks, practice your casting a bit, find some nice water and give yourself the chance to discover a pastime that will reward you with peaceful enjoyment for the rest of your life.

Tight lines!

APPENDIX

Essential Equipment Check List

Rod	☐	Dry flies	☐
Reel	☐	Wet flies	☐
Fly line	☐	Nymphs	☐
Leaders	☐	Streamers	☐
Tippet spools & holder	☐	Split shot	☐
Backing	☐	Strike indicators	☐
Vest or chest pack	☐	Knot tool	☐
Waders and belt	☐	Floatant and holder	☐
Wading shoes	☐	Net and net holder	☐
Wader patch kit	☐	Auto-inflating PFD	☐
Wading staff	☐	Hat	☐
Nippers	☐	Shirts	☐
Forceps	☐	Pants	☐
Fly boxes	☐	Flask	☐
Retractors/zingers	☐		☐
Magnifiers	☐		☐
Polarized sunglasses	☐		☐
Flashlight	☐		☐

ABOUT THE AUTHOR

JERRY O'CONNELL has been fly fishing since he was 12. Having learned the basics on the murky waters of northern New Jersey, he continued to hone his skills as he fished ever-increasingly clear waters in New England, Canada, the Caribbean and New Zealand before eventually settling on—and in—the crystalline rivers of Montana.

Following a career in the software industry in New England, Jerry has become active in the restoration and preservation of Montana's Big Blackfoot River. He founded The Big Blackfoot Riverkeeper program where he is executive director, and is a board member of the Big Blackfoot Chapter Trout Unlimited.

He and his fly fishing wife Deborah, with several dogs and horses, now enjoy a life of quiet solitude in western Montana.

Made in the USA
Middletown, DE
14 May 2022

65764764R00085